Contents

Any words appearing in the text in bold, **like this**, are explained in the glossary.

Electricity is everywhere!

Electricity is part of everyday life. We use electricity dozens of times every day. Without electricity we could not light up a room with the flick of a switch. We could not listen to the radio, CDs, or MP3 players. It would be much more challenging to cook food or to keep food cold. Televisions and computers would not even exist. Our lives would be completely different without electricity.

We use electricity to light our cities.

What is electricity?

Electricity is a form of energy. It is caused by the flow of **electrons**. Electrons are tiny particles that each have a small charge (force). The electrons orbit (circle) around the centre of an **atom**. Atoms are the tiny particles that make up everything in the universe. This book, you, and even the air around you are all made from atoms. The centre of an atom is called the **nucleus**.

An electron can leave its orbit and move to a nearby atom. Each moving electron creates a tiny electrical charge. When huge numbers of electrons all move in the same direction, they make electricity. This electricity can be used to power things such as lights and computers.

DO IT YOURSELF

Electrical Experiments

Electricity and Circuits

Rachel Lynette

www.heinemann.co.uk/library

Visit our website to find out more information about Heinemann Library books.

To order:

☎ Phone 44 (0) 1865 888066

📄 Send a fax to 44 (0) 1865 314091

💻 Visit the Heinemann bookshop at **www.heinemann.co.uk/library** to browse our catalogue and order online.

First published in Great Britain by Heinemann Library, Halley Court, Jordan Hill, Oxford OX2 8EJ, part of Pearson Education.

Heinemann is a registered trademark of Pearson Education Ltd.

© Pearson Education Ltd 2008
First published in paperback in 2008
The moral right of the proprietor has been asserted.

Editorial: Louise Galpine and Kate deVilliers
Design: Richard Parker and Tinstar Design Ltd
Illustrations: Oxford designers & illustrators
Picture Research: Mica Brancic and Hannah Taylor
Production: Victoria Fitzgerald

Originated by Chroma Graphics (Overseas) Pte. Ltd
Printed and bound in China by Leo Paper Group.

ISBN 978 0 431 11127 8 (hardback)
12 11 10 09 08
10 9 8 7 6 5 4 3 2 1

ISBN 978 0 431 11143 8 (paperback)
12 11 10 09 08
10 9 8 7 6 5 4 3 2 1

British Library Cataloguing in Publication Data
Lynette, Rachel
Electrical experiments : electricity and circuits . – (Do it yourself)
537

A full catalogue record for this book is available from the British Library.

Acknowledgements

We would like to thank the following for permission to reproduce photographs: ©Alamy pp. **7** (Westend 61), **10**, (JUPITERIMAGES/Brand X), **14** (Keith van-Loen), **16** (Adrian Muttitt), **17** (John Cole), **23** (Judith Collins), **33** (Leslie Garland Picture Library), **37** (NRT); ©Corbis pp. **31** (The Art Archive), **42** (Najlah Feanny), **43** (Walter Geiersperger), **39**, **41** Corbis Royalty Free; ©Ecoscene pp. **34** (Paul Thompson), **35** (Paul Kennedy**)**; ©Getty Images pp. **15**, **29** right, **40** (Photodisc), **20** (David Woolley), **21** (Jan Stromme); ©Photolibrary.com p. **11** (Darren Bennett); ©Science Photo Library pp. **4** (Rafael Macia), **6** (Sheila Terry), **13** (Simon Lewis), **25** (Cordelia Molloy), **27** (Jesse), **29** left (Volker Steger).

Cover photograph of a close-up of a light bulb reproduced with permission of ©Getty Images/ LOOK/ Hans Georg Merkel.

We would like to thank Ann Fullick for her invaluable help in the preparation of this book.

Every effort has been made to contact copyright holders of any material reproduced in this book. Any omissions will be rectified in subsequent printings if notice is given to the publishers.

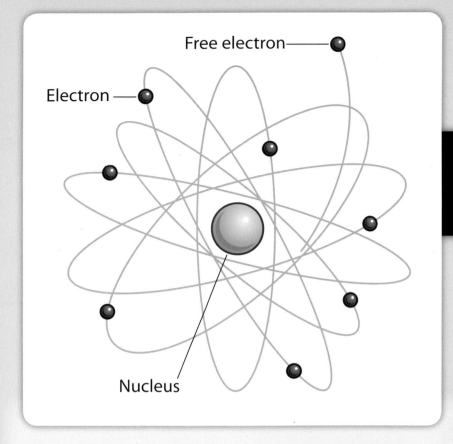

Free electron

Electron

Nucleus

This is a diagram of an atom. Each electron creates a tiny electrical charge.

Safety first!

Electricity is useful, but it can be very dangerous. It is important to follow safety rules when using electricity.

When using electrical sockets, follow these guidelines:
- Never put anything other than a plug into an socket.
- Plug things in carefully, touching only the plastic part of the plug.
- Do not touch damaged wires. Ask an adult to repair or replace them.
- Keep electrical appliances away from water and make sure your hands are dry.

When using batteries, follow these guidelines:
- Never try to break a battery open.
- Do not put a battery in your mouth.
- Dispose of dead batteries properly.

When you are outside, follow these guidelines:
- Go inside during a thunderstorm.
- Do not climb trees or fly kites near power lines.
- If you see a power line on the ground, stay away from it!

Experiments and equipment

All of the experiments in this book are safe, but it is still important to follow instructions carefully. Never experiment with electrical sockets.

You can purchase most of the equipment needed for these experiments at an electronics store. Your electrical equipment may not look quite like the ones in the pictures. For example, some battery holders have wires attached, while others do not. You may need to make adjustments in the experiments to make your equipment work.

The insulation must be stripped from the ends of the wires before they can be used in experiments.

Stripping insulated wire

Many of the experiments in this book use insulated wire. Insulated wire is covered with a plastic coating. You will need to remove this coating from the ends of the wires that you are using. This is called stripping the wire. Ask an adult to use a special tool called a wire stripper to strip your wires.

Attaching wires

Different bulb and battery holders use different methods of attaching wires. Sometimes there is a clip. If you press down on the clip, you can expose a small ring of metal. You can thread your wire through this ring. When you let go of the clip, it secures the wire. Other holders secure the wires with a small screw. For these holders, you will need to bend the end of the wire into a hook shape. Unscrew the screw a few turns with a small screwdriver and slip the wire hook under the screw. Then tighten the screw to secure the wire.

Putting the battery in correctly

A battery has two ends (terminals). One end is positive and the other is negative. Most battery holders are marked with a "+" and a "−" so that you will know which way to place the battery. If your holder is not marked, just remember that the negative end of the battery always goes near the spring in the battery holder. If your battery holder has wires attached, the positive end of your battery goes towards the red wire, while the negative end goes towards the black wire.

Always remember to put the negative end of the battery towards the spring in the battery holder.

Static electricity

Steps to follow

Sticky cereal

For this experiment you will need:

* A balloon

* Breakfast cereal or dry oatmeal. Puffed cereals work especially well.

* Your hair.

1 Blow up the balloon and put a knot in the end.

2 Rub it on your hair in one direction for 10 seconds.

3 Hold the balloon close to the cereal, but don't touch the cereal with it. What happens?

Opposites attract

Why did the cereal stick to the balloon? When you rubbed the balloon on your hair, negatively charged **electrons** travelled from your hair to the balloon. This gave the balloon a negative charge. Negative and positive charges attract each other. The negative charges in the balloon attracted the positive charges in the cereal, so the cereal "jumped" to the balloon! This build-up of charges is called **static electricity**.

You may have noticed that after a while the cereal fell off the balloon. This is because as more and more negatively charged electrons were attracted to the cereal, the cereal took on a negative charge. With both the balloon and the cereal having negative charges, they were no longer attracted to each other. Instead, they **repelled** each other. This means that they pushed away from each other. When the charges are the same, they repel rather than attract.

More static electricity

Try to get more things to stick to your balloon. Do some things work better than others? Can you get your balloon to stick to a wall? What if you try charging your balloon with something other than your hair? Here are some things to try:

- A cotton T-shirt
- A wool sock
- Kitchen paper
- A silk scarf
- A plastic bag.

You probably discovered that some materials worked better than others. This is because the **atoms** in some types of material tend to hold onto their electrons, while the atoms in other types of material tend to let them go. Hair and wool give up electrons much more readily than paper or plastic.

Bending water

Take your balloon into a room with a sink. Turn on the water so that it makes a thin but steady stream. Charge your balloon by rubbing it on your hair. Then hold it close to the stream of water. Were you able to make the water bend? Just like with the cereal, the positive charges in the water are attracted to the negative charges in your balloon.

Static electricity is making this girl's hair stand on end.

Static electricity in our world

Have you ever pulled a woolly hat off your head, only to find that your hair is sticking out in all directions? When you pull off a woolly hat, it rubs against your hair. Negatively charged electrons move to the hat, leaving your hair with a positive charge. Your hair sticks up because each positively charged hair is trying to get as far away from the hairs around it as it can.

Socks often become charged by rubbing against each other in a hot tumble dryer. When you take them out of the dryer, the opposite charges attract each other, so you may find socks stuck together. If they are strongly charged, you may hear a crackling sound or see a spark when you pull them apart.

You can give yourself a charge by shuffling along a carpet wearing socks. You will not feel the charge until you try to touch something metal or another person. If you touch another person, you are both in for a shocking experience!

Lightning

Lightning is really just a big spark! In a thunderstorm, water droplets and ice particles inside clouds rub against each other. The negative charges in the cloud are attracted to positive charges on the ground and in other clouds. When enough negative charges build up, the charges leap to the ground, making the bright flash that we see as lightning.

Lightning is really just static electricity!

Hot lightning

Lightning is extremely hot. A bolt of lightning heats the air around it to over 27,760 °C (50,000 °F). That is over four times hotter than the surface of the Sun!

Insulators and conductors

Steps to follow

Make a conductor detector

For this experiment you will need:

* A D-size battery
* A battery holder
* A small electric buzzer with a black and a red wire attached (available at electronic stores)
* An 20-cm (8-in) piece of insulated wire, with about 1.5 cm (0.5 in) of the insulation stripped off each end
* An assortment of small household objects such as paper clips, pencils, keys, spoons, and marbles.

1 Put the battery into the battery holder. Connect one end of the 20-cm (8-in) wire to the negative end of the battery holder.

2 Connect the end of the red wire on the buzzer to the positive end of the battery holder. Touch the end of the 20-cm (8-in) wire to the end of the black wire on the buzzer to test your buzzer.

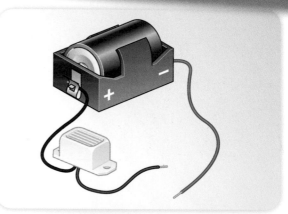

3 Test the items you collected to see which ones will let the electricity flow through them. Select an item and touch the free ends of the two wires to it. **Conductors** will make the buzzer buzz, while **insulators** will not. Separate your conductors and insulators into two groups.

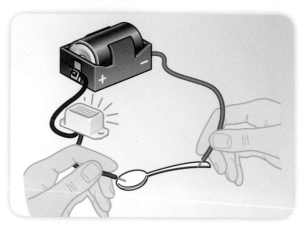

Conducting electricity

When the buzzer buzzed, the battery was forcing the **electrons** in the wires to move from **atom** to atom. This flow of electricity is called a **current**. The path the electricity travels through is called a **circuit**.

Electrical current flows easily through some materials. The electrons in these materials can move from one atom to another. These materials are called conductors. Most metals are conductors, which is why wire is made from metal. Did you notice that all of the conductors you tested were made from metal or had metal on them? Water is also a conductor, but you should never experiment with water and electricity.

Insulators are the opposite of conductors. They do not allow electricity to flow through them. The electrons in these materials do not move easily from one atom to another. Most non-metal materials, such as glass, plastic, wood, and rubber, are insulators.

These wires are made of copper because copper is a good conductor.

Parts of a circuit

Every circuit must have three parts:

- A **power source**: The power source provides the electricity. In your circuit the power source is the battery. The power source for the circuits in your home is a **generator** in a power plant.

- An **output device**: The output device is the object that the electricity powers. In your circuit, the output device is the buzzer. The electricity makes it buzz. You have many output devices in your home. Lights, televisions, ovens, blenders, and hair dryers are all output devices. How many output devices can you see around you right now?

- **Connectors**: Connectors connect the power source to the output device. In your circuit, the connectors are the wires. The connectors that bring electricity to your home are the power lines that carry electricity from the power plant to your neighbourhood.

There are many types of output device.

Large transmission lines can carry up to half a million volts of electricity!

High voltage

Look at your battery. Can you work out how many **volts** it has? A volt is a measure of the pressure (force) of electricity. One way to think about volts is to imagine a garden hose. If the water is turned on just a little, there is not much force, and this force cannot push the water very far. A D-size battery has 1.5 volts of electricity. With only 1.5 volts, your battery is like a hose with just a trickle of water coming out.

The sockets in your wall have quite a bit more voltage than a battery. Sockets have 120 volts of electricity. Everything that plugs in runs on 120 volts. Imagine the hose again, but this time the water is turned on full blast! Appliances and electronics need more force to make them work.

The power lines outside have even higher voltage. Large **transmission lines** can carry up to half a million volts! This time, instead of imagining a garden hose, imagine the hose on a fire engine. Transmission lines need to carry so many volts because the force must be strong enough to be pushed over many kilometres from the power plant to your neighbourhood.

Power line safety

Electricity always takes the easiest path to the ground. That is why it is important to keep anything that is touching the ground away from anything that has a high voltage, such as power lines. You should never fly a kite near a power line. If the kite touches the line, the electricity can use the kite and the string to get to the ground. Since you are holding the string and standing on the ground, it will also use you! You can be shocked, burned, or even killed by the electricity in a power line.

It is also important not to climb trees that are near power lines. Even though trees are made of wood, and wood is an insulator, trees have water inside them. Electricity can use the water inside the tree as well as any water or dirt on the tree as a conductor to reach the ground. The tree does not even have to be touching the power line to be dangerous. Electricity can arc (jump) to a nearby tree to get to the ground.

Never climb trees near power lines!

Birds on the line

Birds can safely perch on power lines because they are not touching the ground. Electricity therefore cannot use them to get to the ground. Electricity always takes the easiest path. It is easier for electricity to go through the power line than it is for it to go through the bird.

If a nearby branch on a tree were to touch a bird while it was perched on a power line, the electricity would zip through the bird to the tree and down to the ground. The bird would end up dead from electrocution.

Birds can safely perch on power lines.

Open and closed circuits

Steps to follow

1
Twist the exposed 8 cm (3 in) on the long insulated wire into a closed loop. Be sure that the insulated wire is not part of the loop. The loop should be big enough to put your finger through.

2
Put the battery in the battery holder. Connect the non-looped end of the long insulated wire to the negative end of the battery holder.

3
Connect the red wire on the buzzer to the positive end of the battery holder.

Make a steady-hand game

For this experiment you will need:
* A D-size battery
* A battery holder
* A small electric buzzer with a black and a red wire attached
* A 60-cm (2-foot) piece of insulated wire, with about 5 cm (2 in) stripped from one end and 8 cm (3 in) stripped from the other end
* A 60-cm (2-foot) piece of stiff (but bendable) uninsulated wire
* Tape
* A heavy book
* An unsharpened pencil.

4 Bend the uninsulated wire so that it has some curves. The curvier you make the wire, the harder your game will be. Twist the stripped end of the black wire from the buzzer onto one end of the curvy wire. You may need to tape it to keep it secure.

5 Position the curvy wire so that most of it extends over the edge of a table. Put a book on top of the end that is connected to the buzzer to hold it in place.

6 See how steady your hand is by trying to move the wire loop from one end of the curvy wire to the other end without touching it. If the wire loop touches the curvy wire, your buzzer will buzz!

How does the game work?

When you set up this game, you create an **open circuit**. An open circuit is a **circuit** in which the electricity cannot flow. The set-up for the game is an open circuit because there is a space between the curvy wire and the battery. This means the electricity cannot flow. But when you make a mistake in the game and the wire loop touches the curvy wire, the circuit is completed and the buzzer buzzes. A circuit through which electricity can flow is called a **closed circuit**.

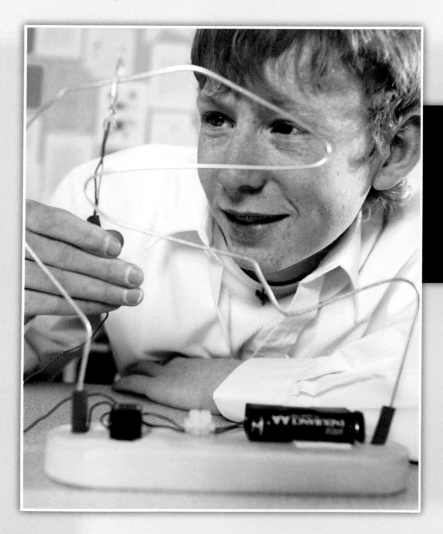

You can make your steady-hand game harder by adding more curves to the curvy wire or by making the wire loop smaller.

Take a look around you. How many of the **output devices** you see are on open circuits and how many are on closed circuits? If you are reading this book with a lamp, that lamp is on a closed circuit. If there is a television in the room and it is turned off, then it is on an open circuit.

Improving the game

You can also add a handle to the wire loop by taping the part of the wire that is near the loop to an unsharpened pencil. Be sure to tape along the whole length of the pencil.

Switches

We use switches to open and close circuits. The most common switches are for lights, but we also use switches on appliances and toys to turn them on and off. On a light switch, when the switch is in the "on" position, a thin metal strip keeps the circuit closed. Turning the switch to the "off" position moves the metal strip and opens the circuit.

A switch works by opening and closing the circuit.

Push-button switches

The first light switches were made back in the late 1800s. They had two buttons to push instead of one to press. Pushing one button would close the circuit to turn on the light, while pushing the other button would open it to turn off the light.

Batteries and bulbs

Steps to follow

1 Put the bulb in the bulb holder and the battery in the battery holder.

2 Connect one end of one of the wires to the battery holder. Connect the other end to the bulb holder. Use the second wire to connect the other side of the bulb holder to the other side of the battery holder. Your bulb should light up!

Make a bulb light

For this experiment you will need:

* A D-size battery
* A battery holder
* A small bulb like the type that goes in a torch
* A bulb holder
* Three pieces of 20-cm (8-in) insulated wire, with about 1.5 cm (0.5 in) of the insulation stripped off each end
* A switch (these are commonly called knife switches, although they are not sharp!)

3 You can add a switch to your circuit to turn your bulb on and off. Disconnect one of the wires and connect the switch. Connect the third wire to the other end of the switch. Connect the other end of this third wire to the battery or the bulb holder to make a loop.

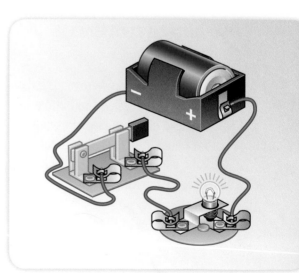

If your bulb did not light, try these suggestions for fixing it:

- Make sure your bulb is screwed in properly. The bottom of the bulb must touch the bottom of the bulb holder.

- Make sure the exposed metal ends of your wires are making contact with the metal connectors on the battery and bulb holder.

- Make sure your bulb is not damaged or burned out.

How does it work?

The circuit you built is called a **simple circuit** because it has just one **power source** and one **output device**. The electricity travels continuously around the loop to light the bulb. When you added the switch, you were able to easily open and close the circuit.

Speedy electricity

Electricity travels very quickly. Blink your eyes. In the time it took you to blink once, electricity can travel all the way around the Earth!

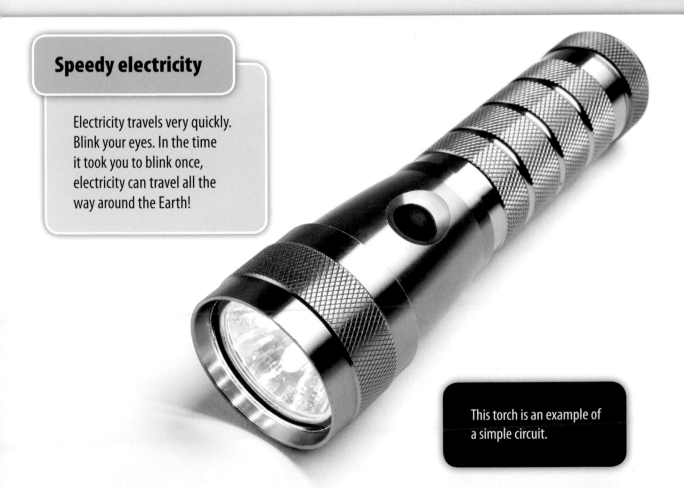

This torch is an example of a simple circuit.

Make a lighted house

For this experiment you will need:

* Four D-size batteries
* Four battery holders
* Three small bulbs like the type that go in a torch
* Three bulb holders
* Seven 20-cm (8-in) insulated wires, with about 1.5 cm (0.5 in) of the insulation stripped off each end
* Three small boxes without lids; try small, clean milk cartons with the tops cut off
* Scissors
* Paint (optional).

1 The three boxes will be the houses. Cut holes in them to make windows. The bottom of the box will be the roof. You can paint them to make them look more like real houses if you want.

2 Use wires to connect four batteries in a row. Position them so that positive and negative ends are connected. If you connect two like ends, your circuit will not work. One way to make sure you get this right is to line them up so all the positive ends are facing in one direction.

3 Add the three light bulbs to the circuit. Your batteries and bulbs should be connected in one big loop. Your bulbs should all be lit.

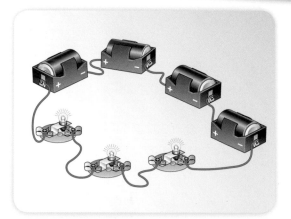

4 Put a box over each light bulb. Turn off the lights in the room and see the windows of your houses glow!

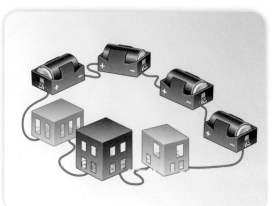

One path

The circuit you made to light up your houses is called a **series circuit**. Series circuits can have multiple power sources and output devices. In a series circuit, there is only one loop (path) for the electricity to take. Everything in the circuit is on that path.

What do you think will happen if you unscrew just one of the bulbs? Try it and see. The other two bulbs went out because all the bulbs are on the same loop. When you unscrewed the bulb, you opened the circuit so that none of the other bulbs could get electricity from the battery.

Party lights used to be wired in series so that if one bulb burned out, all the lights went out.

Rewire your model houses

You can wire the houses you made in a different way so that if one bulb is removed or turned off, the other bulbs stay on. This time, use just one battery. Start by making a simple circuit. Then use two wires to add a second bulb onto the first bulb holder. Add the third bulb to the second bulb holder.

In a parallel circuit each output device has its own path back to the power source.

Battery

Bulb holder

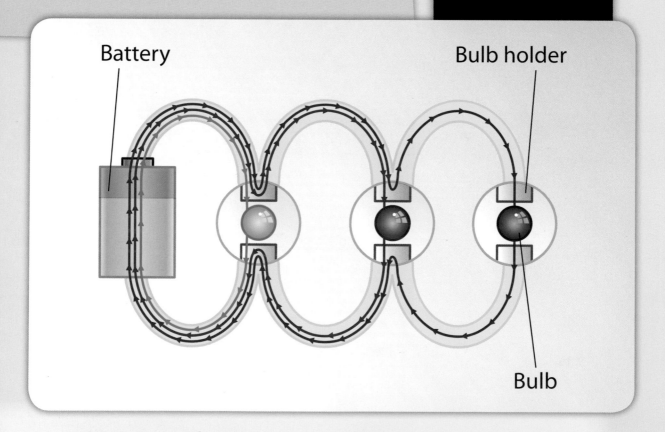

Bulb

Multiple paths

Your houses are now on a **parallel circuit**. In a parallel circuit there are multiple paths through which the electricity can flow. This is because each output device has its own path back to the power source. Now if you unscrew one bulb, the others will stay lit. Can you work out how to add a switch into your circuit that turns off just one light?

Wiring your box houses with a parallel circuit is more like the wiring we use in real life. Almost all buildings are wired with parallel circuits. That is why you can turn off the light in your bedroom and the other lights in your home will stay on.

Printed circuit boards

Today **printed circuit boards (PCBs)** are often used instead of bulky wires in many kinds of electronics. Most PCBs are made by covering the entire board with a thin layer of copper and then stripping away the copper that is not needed to make connections. The electricity travels over the copper pathways that are left.

Printed circuit boards, like this one, can be found in computers, music players, and other electronics.

To share or not to share

Another difference between series and parallel circuits is how they use the power source. In a series circuit, the power source is shared by all the bulbs in the loop. That is why you used a lot of batteries to light the houses you made. If you had tried to use just one battery, the bulbs would have been very dim.

In a parallel circuit, each bulb has its own path back to the power source. This means that each bulb gets the full strength of the battery. That is why you were able to use just one battery to light three bulbs.

How a light bulb works

The bulbs that you have been using are called **incandescent bulbs**. Incandescent bulbs contain a thin wire called a **filament**. See if you can find the filament in one of your bulbs. When electricity flows through the filament, it makes the filament so hot that it glows. All the light in an incandescent bulb comes from that glowing filament.

Electricity travels through the lead wires into the filament to make the light bulb glow.

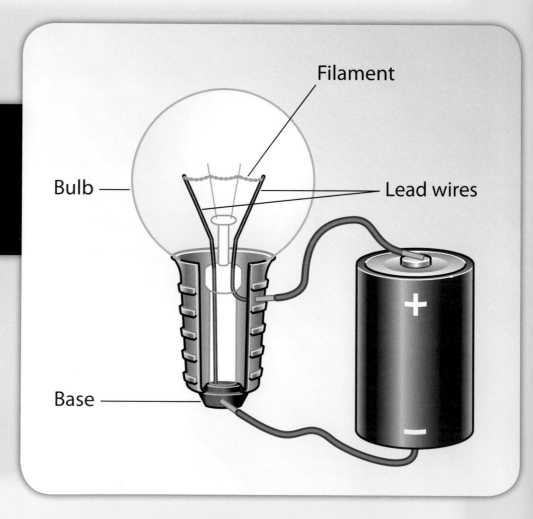

Filament

Bulb

Lead wires

Base

Inside your bulb the lead wires carry electricity to the filament. The lead wires are connected to different parts of the **base**. One of the lead wires is connected to the bottom of the base. The other one is connected to the side of the base. In order to complete the circuit, electricity must be able to flow into both the side and bottom of the base.

Other types of bulb

Incandescent bulbs are just one way to use electricity to make light. Many people have replaced their incandescent bulbs with compact fluorescent lamps (CFLs). Instead of using a filament, CFLs contain small amounts of mercury in gas form. When electricity flows through the gas, light is emitted.

CFLs are popular because they use much less electricity than incandescent bulbs, which saves people money on their electricity bills. However, some people are concerned about the mercury fumes inside the lamp. Mercury is a toxic metallic element that can cause health problems if it is ingested or inhaled. It is important to be careful not to break a CFL and to dispose of it properly when it burns out.

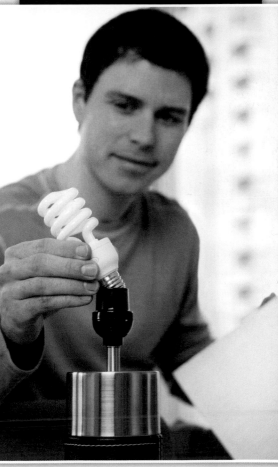

CFLs, like this one, use much less electricity than incandescent bulbs.

LEDs use even less electricity than CFLs.

Light emitting diodes (LEDs) are another way to make light with electricity. LEDs are especially good for making coloured light. LEDs last for a long time and use very little electricity. However, they do not produce much light. To make a lot of light, many LEDs must be used, and that can be expensive. LEDs can be found in some torches and in the displays on electronic equipment. They are also used in traffic lights.

Making electricity

Steps to follow

1 Mix several tablespoons of salt into the warm water. It is okay if some of the salt does not mix in.

2 Trace a penny on the kitchen paper and cut out six penny-sized circles from the kitchen paper.

3 Tape one wire to a penny and put the penny, wire side down, on a plate. Dip one kitchen paper circle into the saltwater. Place it on the penny. Then put a 10p piece on the kitchen paper circle.

4 Repeat the pattern – penny, wet kitchen paper circle, 10p piece, penny, wet kitchen paper circle – until you are out of coins.

5 Dry off your fingers and the 10p piece at the top of the stack. Carefully tape the second wire to the 10p piece.

Make a battery

For this experiment you will need:

* Six pennies
* Six 10p pieces
* Kitchen paper
* Warm water in a cup
* Salt
* A pencil
* Scissors
* Two 20-cm (8-in) insulated wires, with about 1.5 cm (0.5 in) of the insulation stripped off each end
* Tape
* A small plate or saucer
* Headphones.

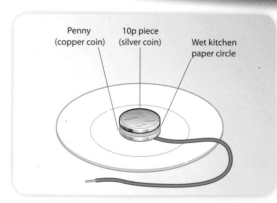

Penny (copper coin)　10p piece (silver coin)　Wet kitchen paper circle

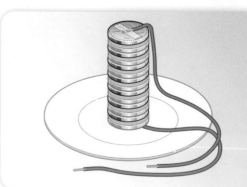

The first battery

The battery you just made is similar to the first battery that was ever made. In 1799 Italian physicist Alessandro Volta alternated large discs of copper, zinc, and cardboard soaked in brine (saltwater) to make the first battery. Volta's invention was called the **Volta Pile**.

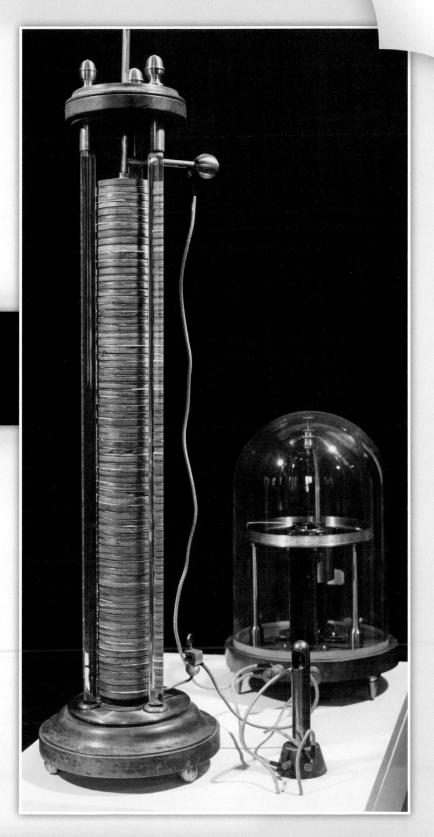

This is the first electric battery invented by Alessandro Volta in 1799.

The Volta Pile works because the copper loses **electrons** to the saltwater, while the zinc gains electrons from it. This causes an electric **current** to travel from one end of the pile to the other. The Volta Pile was the first invention to provide a steady supply of electricity. Volta experimented with his pile by using different types of metal and liquid and by making his piles taller. He even connected several piles together to increase the voltage. Volta's work was so important that the **volt** was named after him!

Try your Volta Pile

1. To test the battery, wrap the exposed end of one of the wires around the headphone jack.

2. Put on the headphones and rub the other wire along the edge of the jack.

3. You should hear a crackling sound. This crackling is the battery turning electricity into sound!

More with the Volta Pile

You can measure the amount of volts your battery has by using a voltmeter. You will need to use one that measures very small amounts of electricity — less than a volt.

If you make your pile higher with more coins, you can increase the voltage. You can also experiment with different metals. Try different coins, washers, and circles of kitchen foil. Just make sure that the two metals that you use are different. You can also try vinegar or lemon juice instead of saltwater.

Fruit power

A popular experiment involves using a lemon to make a low-voltage battery. To make a lemon battery, gently squeeze a fresh lemon to release the juices. Then insert two different types of small metal objects into the lemon. They should be about 2.5 centimetres (one inch) apart. Make sure that some of the metal is sticking out of the lemon. It works best if one of the types of metal is copper. You could use a copper penny or a small piece of stripped wire. For the other metal, you could use a paper clip, a nail, or a different coin.

You can make a low-voltage battery from a lemon. These lemon batteries are powering a digital clock.

You can test your lemon battery by hooking it up to a voltmeter. You can also touch both pieces of metal with your tongue. You should feel a faint tingle. (It is fine to test a lemon battery with your tongue, but you should NEVER test a real battery that way.)

Modern batteries do not look like the Volta Pile or a piece of fruit, but the basic principle is the same. Just like the Volta Pile and the lemon battery, today's batteries use two different types of metal and a liquid **conductor**.

Beyond batteries

Batteries are great when you do not need very many volts. But when you need more volts, you need a stronger **power source**. Large **generators** at a power plant can create a great deal of electricity.

In a generator, magnets are used to create a powerful **magnetic field**. This magnetic field interacts with a conductor – usually coils of copper wire. A force is applied to the magnets or the conductors in order to make them move. This movement creates an electrical current in the conductor. In this way, generators turn motion into electrical energy.

Cow pat power!

Scientists have discovered that dried cow dung can be burned to generate electricity! Some farmers are using cow dung to power their farm machinery.

This power plant is generating a great deal of electricity.

Turbines

A generator only works when the magnets or conductors are moving. This motion is created by spinning a **turbine**. A turbine usually consists of blades attached to a shaft. Water, wind, or steam are used to spin the turbine.

Most power plants use steam-driven turbines. In most cases the steam comes from burning **fossil fuels** such as coal. The burning coal heats water to make steam. The steam is pushed through a pipe so that it is under a lot of pressure when it hits the turbine, making it spin fast! Just over one-third of the electricity generated in the United Knigdom comes from burning coal. Unfortunately, burning coal causes a great deal of pollution. In addition, coal is a **non-renewable** resource. It takes millions of years for Earth to make coal, so once it is all gone, it cannot be replaced.

This is the largest wind farm in New Zealand.

Fortunately, there are other ways to spin the turbine on a generator. Wind can be used to turn giant turbines. Often many wind turbines are built together on wind farms. For **hydroelectric energy**, water is used to spin the turbine. A newer technology involves using the power of the ocean's tides to spin giant underwater turbines. Wind and hydroelectric energy are good examples of **renewable**, non-polluting ways to generate electricity.

The energy we use

Steps to follow

1 Plug the wire that came with your generator into the appropriate place on the generator. (If your generator has a place to screw in a bulb, do not use it for this experiment.) The wire should split into two parts, each with a clip on the end. Connect these clips to your bulb holder.

2 Turn the handle of the generator gently. The light should go on! Be careful not to jerk the handle or spin it too quickly. This will cause your bulb to burn out.

3 Now try adding more bulbs to your circuit. Can you use the generator to light all three bulbs?

Using a generator

For this experiment you will need:

* A handheld **generator** with a handle that you turn (it should come with a wire)
* Three small bulbs
* Three bulb holders
* Two 20-cm (8-in) insulated wires, with about 1.5 cm (0.5 in) of the insulation stripped off each end.

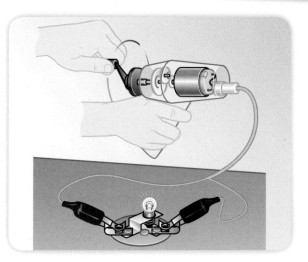

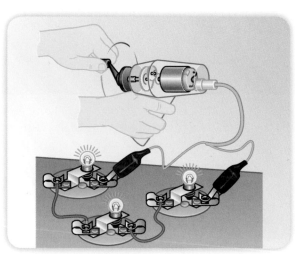

How does it work?

Your handheld generator can light a bulb because you are supplying the power! The handle on the generator is like a **turbine**. When you turn the handle, you are making the movement that is needed to spin the magnets or the coils of copper wire inside the generator. You are turning your motion energy into electrical energy!

You turn motion energy into electrical energy when you turn the handle on this wind-up radio.

More with your handheld generator

When you added more bulbs to your circuit, you probably wired them in one big loop to make a **series circuit**. Ask a friend to unscrew one of the bulbs while you turn the handle of the generator. Did all of the bulbs go out?

See if you can change your circuit to make it a **parallel circuit**. You will need extra wires to do this. Remember, in a parallel circuit, each bulb will have its own path back to the **power source**. You will know that your circuit is wired in parallel if the other bulbs stay lit as you unscrew one of the bulbs while your friend turns the handle.

Hydroelectric energy

Your handheld generator is not that different from the generators at a **hydroelectric energy** plant. Of course, the generators at a hydroelectric energy plant are much bigger. The water for a hydroelectric energy plant comes from a large river. A dam is built across the river so that the water can be stored behind the dam in a reservoir. This water is released into a large pipe called a **penstock**. Gravity makes the water move quickly, so that by the time it hits the turbine, the force is very powerful.

At a hydroelectric plant, water is used to generate electricity.

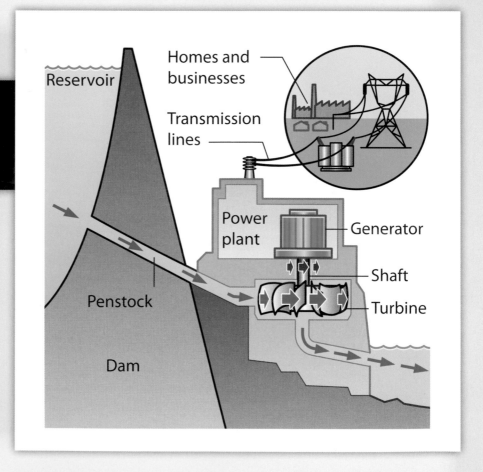

The turbines in a hydroelectric energy plant are very big. Some of the largest turbines can weigh up to 156 tonnes (172 tons). That is heavier than 28 elephants! It takes a huge amount of water to spin these giant turbines. The force of the water makes them spin quickly – up to 90 **revolutions** per minute. Each turbine is connected to a shaft that also spins. It is this spinning that makes the magnets move inside the generator to make electricity. Twenty percent of the electricity generated on Earth comes from hydroelectric energy!

Transmitting electricity

Once the electricity is generated, it is carried to factories, cities, and houses. At first it is carried in high voltage **transmission lines**. These are the large lines that you see suspended on metal towers across the countryside. The electricity that flows through them is very high voltage because it must be pushed over long distances. The voltage is decreased (stepped down) at a **substation**. From the substation, electricity travels through smaller **distribution lines**. Usually these are strung on poles, but sometimes they are underground. These lines carry the electricity to your home. The last stop that electricity makes before it enters your home is the **pole transformer**. The pole transformer steps down the voltage one more time so that the electricity can safely travel through the wires in your home.

Hydroelectric energy leaders

Canada produces more hydroelectric energy than any other country. Norway produces enough hydroelectric energy to meet 99 percent of its electricity needs.

The turbines at hydroelectric power plants are very large.

Too much electricity

People in industrialized countries use a great deal of electricity. Burning **fossil fuels** to make electricity causes pollution. Many people are concerned because pollution contributes to **global warming**. This means that generating electricity from fossil fuels is causing climate changes on our planet. Even though some electricity is generated using clean, **renewable** resources, the majority of power is still generated from fossil fuels such as coal and oil. By **conserving** energy, you can help make our planet a cleaner, healthier place to live.

Industrialized countries use a lot of electricity.

Ways to conserve energy

- Turn off lights when you leave a room.
- Ask your parents to switch from **incandescent bulbs** to CFLs. These use only a quarter as much electricity for the same amount of light!
- Don't leave things such as TVs and stereos on when you are not using them.
- In the winter, put on a jumper instead of turning up the heat.
- Keep doors and windows shut when the weather is cold.
- Take shorter showers.
- Run only full loads of dishes and clothes. Use energy-saver settings.
- Don't keep the refrigerator or freezer open any longer than necessary.
- When your parents are buying new appliances, ask them to buy ones with the Energy Saving Recommended logo. These appliances are made to save energy!
- Try not to use a lot of disposable items such as paper plates and plastic water bottles. The factories that produce these things use electricity to power their machines. A lot of electricity is used to make products that are only used once before they are thrown away.
- Recycle paper, bottles, cans, and plastic containers instead of throwing them away. Recycling not only keeps rubbish out of landfills, it also saves electricity. It takes much less electricity to make products from recycled materials than it does from scratch. Recycling just one aluminium can or glass bottle saves enough electricity to power a light bulb for four hours!

Recycling is a good way to conserve energy!

A powerful future

Electricity is an important part of our lives. Every year more and more electronic devices are invented. In addition, in underdeveloped countries more people are using electricity than ever before. All this electricity use is putting a drain on our natural resources and polluting our planet.

With rising awareness of **global warming**, people are starting to **conserve** more electricity. If everyone did just a few things to save energy, it could have a huge impact on our world.

These people need electricity to make their electronic devices work.

Green energy

Renewable, non-polluting sources of energy are sometimes called **green energy**. In order to continue to use electricity, people will have to learn to use more green energy instead of **fossil fuels**. In addition to wind and **hydroelectric energy**, there are other sources of green energy.

Solar energy uses energy from the Sun to generate electricity. Some people use large solar collectors to power their homes. In the future, many more people may use solar power. **Geothermal energy** comes from heat under the surface of Earth. This heat is released as steam that can be used to spin **turbines**.

This house has solar panels that convert energy from the Sun into electricity.

One problem with most types of renewable energy is that they are still more expensive than fossil fuels. For example, a wind turbine is a large and very expensive machine. Not only does it cost a lot to build, but it also costs a lot to keep it in working order. Electricity from wind costs more than electricity from coal. But for many people, knowing that their electricity comes from green energy is worth the extra cost. Although it is expensive now, one day green energy may be less expensive than fossil fuels. Maybe one day all of our energy will be green.

Glossary

atom extremely tiny particle. Atoms make up all things. If all the atoms in a grain of sand were pennies, you would have enough money to give each person on the planet over £500 billion.

base metal part of an incandescent bulb that screws into a socket. The base of a light bulb conducts electricity into wires that lead to the filament.

circuit route around which electrical current can flow. You can put many bulbs on one circuit.

closed circuit uninterrupted path of conductors through which electrical current can flow. When you are listening to the radio, electrical current is flowing through a closed circuit to make the sound.

conductor material that allows electricity to pass through it. The tip of a pencil is a conductor – try it with your battery and see!

connector wire or other material that joins a power source to an output device. If you do not have any wires, you can use strips of aluminium foil as connectors.

conserve use something sparingly so that you do not run out. You can conserve electricity by turning off computer equipment at night.

current flow of electrons through a circuit of conductors. You can stop a current by opening a circuit.

distribution line power line that carries electricity from a substation to buildings and homes. If you see a distribution line on the ground after a storm, don't touch it!

electron tiny charged particle that circles around the centre of an atom. Electrons that are all moving in one direction make an electrical current.

filament thin wire in an incandescent bulb that heats up and glows when an electric current flows through it. A filament can heat up to 2,482 °C (4,500 °F).

fossil fuel fuel formed millions of years ago from decaying plants and animals. Fossil fuels such as coal and oil are non-renewable resources.

generator machine that converts motion into electrical energy. You can see very large generators at hydroelectric energy plants.

geothermal energy energy from the heat that comes from the core of the Earth. Geothermal energy can be used to spin a turbine to make electricity.

global warming increase in the overall temperature of the atmosphere that is believed to be caused by pollution. Burning fossil fuels contributes to global warming.

green energy non-polluting, renewable sources of energy. Many people are interested in powering their homes with green energy.

hydroelectric energy method of producing electricity with the energy of moving water. Hydroelectric energy does not cause pollution.

incandescent bulb light that uses electricity to make a filament glow. Thomas Edison invented the incandescent bulb in 1879.

insulator material that prevents the passage of electricity. If an insulator gets wet, it will become a conductor.

magnetic field space around a magnet in which a magnetic force acts. Powerful magnetic fields are used to generate electricity.

non-renewable something that will run out and cannot be replaced. Oil and coal are non-renewable resources.

nucleus centre of an atom. Electrons orbit the nucleus.

open circuit path of conductors that has been interrupted by a gap so that electric current cannot flow. If your light bulb does not glow, it could be because a wire is loose, causing an open circuit.

output device tool, toy, or appliance that electricity powers. Keep output devices that plug into sockets away from water!

parallel circuit circuit that has two or more paths through which electricity can flow. You can design a parallel circuit with a switch for each light bulb.

penstock channel or pipe used to control the flow of water

pole transformer box on a power pole that steps down the voltage before electricity enters the wires of a house or building. Can you find the pole transformer near your home?

power source battery or generator. A mobile phone uses a rechargeable battery for its power source.

printed circuit board (PCB) flat board that holds electronic components in layers that are connected with copper paths. Ask an adult to take apart an old piece of electronic equipment so you can see the printed circuit board inside.

renewable something that does not run out or that can be replaced easily. Solar power is renewable because we will never run out of sunlight.

repel force that pushes objects away from each other

revolution single turn or rotation

series circuit circuit with only one path (loop) through which the electric current can flow. In a series circuit, if one of the bulbs breaks, all the bulbs stop working.

simple circuit circuit with only one power source and one output device. A buzzer and battery is an example of a simple circuit.

solar energy method of producing electricity with energy from the Sun

static electricity energy that is created between objects that have opposite electrical charges. You can use static electricity to make your hair stick out by charging your comb on a woollen sock before combing your hair.

substation place where voltage from power lines is decreased. You should never try to go inside a substation.

transmission line power line that brings electricity from a substation to buildings and houses. If you do not see transmission lines in your neighbourhood, it is because they are underground.

turbine machine with blades that spin to produce electricity. A wind turbine can have blades that are about 65 metres (215 feet) long.

volt measure of electrical pressure or force. You can increase the volts in a circuit by adding more batteries.

Volta Pile device that uses a stack of different metals, separated by a liquid chemical conductor, to produce a flow of electrons. The taller you make a Volta Pile, the more volts it will have.

Find out more

Books

Charging About: The Story of *Electricity (Science Works)*, Jacqui Bailey
(A&C Black, 2004)

Lots of facts and useful websites.

DK Eyewitness Books: *Electricity*, Steve Parker and Laura Buller
(DK Children, 2005)

Colourful photos and informative text take readers on a journey of the history
of electricity.

Electricity (Young Scientists Investigate), Malcolm Dixon
(Evans Brothers, 2005)

Activities, illustrations and experiments.

Energy Essentials: *Renewable Energy*, Nigel Saunders and Steven
Chapman (Raintree, 2005)

A colourful and informative exploration of alternative energy.

Websites

www.energysavingtrust.org.uk/commit/
This site aims to encourage people to save energy and provides tips on
how to do it.

www.defra.gov.uk/environment/climatechange/index.htm
The Department for Environment, Food, and Rural Affairs' website on
Climate change and energy offers the latest information about energy
use and its effects.

www.sciencemuseum.org.uk
The Science Museum's website offers great information on electricity,
including questions and answers with museum experts.

Places to visit

Pitlochry Hydro Electric Visitors' Centre
Pitlochry Power Station
Perth and Kinross
Perthshire
PH16 5ND
Tel: 01796 473152

The centre has interactive exhibits telling the history of hydro power in Scotland from the 1940s to the present day.

Museum of Electricity
The Old Power Station
Bargates
Christchurch
Dorset
BH23 1QE
Tel: 01202 480467

The museum is set in an Edwardian power station and has hands-on exhibits and demonstrations.

Amberley Working Museum
Amberley Working Museum is situated in West Sussex on the B2139 midway between Arundel and Storrington, adjacent to Amberley railway station.
Tel: 01798 831370

www.amberleymuseum.co.uk/index2.html

See a wide range of exciting electrical equipment at this fascinating open air industrial museum.

Index